HAIKU MASTER

BY
ERIK THOMAS

Listen To The Haiku Master Audiobook:

Sognarr.bandcamp.com

Find Me Online:

SOGNARR

Sognarr Eclipse

Facebook.com/takethejoystick

Twitter.com/ErikDannyThomas

Soundcloud.com/sognarr

Email/sognarr@gmail.com

HAIKU Master
by Erik Thomas

Art, photos, and text, Copyright © 2016 by Erik Thomas
All rights reserved.

No part of this book may be reproduced or transmitted in any form or by any means, electronic or mechanical, including photocopying, recording, or by any information storage and retrieval system, without permission in writing from the copyright owner.

Published by GoPublish, an imprint of Visual Adjectives

GoPublish
14280 Military Trail, #7501
Delray Beach, FL 33482

Library of Congress Control Number: 2016954502

ISBN-13: 978-1-941901-23-6
ISBN-10: 1-941901-23-9

TABLE OF CONTENT

AUTUMN
Powerless
Temptations of a Child
Ingenious Insight
I would rather been a Caveman with a Playstation 2
Proper Balance

WINTER
The Nightmare Song
Guys Like Me
In the End, It Is Feeling That Counts
Pieces for Jo
Sognarr #1 AKA I Want it To Come Natural
Via txt Msg
My Phoenix

SPRING
This Tryst
Him and Her
Metaphorical Way of Perceiving Your Current Dilemma
Grey
2 Flew

SUMMER
Intergalactic
You Say "Your Writings Are So Perfect"
At which Point
Novice and Goddess

"I'll be there to have some fun, on the day the moon blocks out the sun."

ACKNOWLEDGMENTS

FIRST & FOREMOST
MOM & DAD, SANDRA & EARL, ALL MY LOVE
SPECIAL THANKS GO OUT TO MY UNCLE J.J.
From Maxwell Houle
In Loving Memory of Joe!

I just want to thank Big Chris for making sure I would always have a voice and mind of my own.

I want to thank Ches Kanno for inspiring me to travel and write.

Thank you Kelli and Lil Chris the most for keeping my head in the game when I thought I wanted to give everything up!

From Sognarr with Love to all my Fennell family members on the West Coast. Especially Mikey, Kevin & Richard for helping my parents raise me.

CLOVER LEAVES FOREVER.
Neon Bros for Life
Elite Family

–Erik Thomas

Listen To The Haiku Master Audiobook:
Sognarr.bandcamp.com

Find Me Online:
SOGNARR
Sognarr Eclipse

Facebook.com/takethejoystick
Twitter.com/ErikDannyThomas
Soundcloud.com/sognarr
Email/sognarr@gmail.com

Autumn

*Red rose, dead poet
Death by sweater weather wind
Blood thin brain frozen*

POWERLESS

WOULD YOU RATHER EAT THE RED PILL OR THE BLUE PILL?

HAIKU MASTER

Powerless to alter my own eternity,
Hands tied behind my back waiting patiently
As time inconsequentially tortures me with another face smack

Yeah

Unspoken considerations result negatively as the light shines through
I wouldn't take a second back
You were too good to be true

Autumn

Red rose, dead poet
Death by sweater weather wind
Blood thin brain frozen

TEMPTATIONS OF A CHILD

WHY DO PEOPLE IN A FIRST WORLD COUNTRY, TREAT EACH OTHER SO POORLY, BITCH, WHINE AND CARRY ON LIKE THEY HAVE THIRD WORLD PROBLEMS?

HAIKU MASTER

Is it an irresistible urge that makes us do things? I'm not sure but all I know is one thing
No matter who it is that tells you how to do things
It's yourself that will help you to get through things
Me? Well I guess I'm a little hard headed I purposely cross and mix my synonyms and antonyms just to make the outside world think what's wrong with him?
I'll wear a blue sock and a red sock shave my head into a Mohawk ill even switch the jams in a hip hop club to hard rock! Try Me!
I may be a little crazy, that's probably a way to describe me but when I want it I get it
I go over the proper rule of my parents sometimes
But I guess it's worth it in my eyes
Because if everything was civilized
and everyone had mediocre or
average lives they are too ennui
If no one cries
When no one lies
When winners don't try
When there's no celebrities to be scandalized
When there's just the right amount of salt in your chili cheese fries
And I'd hate to say but if no one dies
I guess that's how it is in everyone's lives or at least in mines
I mean, what would the world be if there was an absence of lying, cheating, deceiving heartbreaking I'm sure it would ruin my life so I'm taking these notes down
And stating that I want it all!
I'm saying you have to get a rush to get a thrill in life everyone that stays within the laws
I'm sure it won't last long
You see what it would be if that one guy didn't commit that one crime at least one time
Nobody would take after him so life would be the same for some time
Until that bright idea of taking the clothes off of the rack and tucking them up under your shirt!
Well you got away with it so try again take two things in fact
Like I said I should have bet you like the thrill so of course you come back
For a third a fourth a fifth, until you're trapped
But the allure of what would happen if you didn't get caught that my friends
Is the motivation of a true temptation that is why
The temptations of a child are such a factor in the world today

Autumn

Red rose, dead poet
Death by sweater weather wind
Blood thin brain frozen

INGENIOUS INSIGHT

WOULD YOU EVER FUCK A HANDICAP GIRL?

These are the pretentious thoughts of pathetic men weeping
over loves long lost
Id rather lose an arm than her they'd say
Id trade my health wealth and good fortunes for her love they'd say
Her face as gentle as that of a resting infant her eyes my resting place
For I have died in them 1,000 times upon meeting her
Her body, with strides of mystery and a personality to match
She is the epitome of phenomenal woman
..In my eyes with the loss of a loved one might I shed a single tear, but with the encounter of a new lady, may my desire for a finer love pass.. my attention is hers
Id hate to admit it but Ms New Booty got a nice tush + waist
NICE Tush + Waist? Nice tush and waist? G get ur mind off T + A
Please please someone anyone tell him to his face that poetry is about revolution, relationships, diplomacy, derision, relaxation and race
Revolutions and diplomats? Diplomats and race?
Cant you people see that's what made me a basket case?? What
So I'm only "poetic" if I claim our political system is a disgrace based on the ways of
President George Hitler and his motherfucking master race
Or how about a taste of diplomatic strategy, ill slide you notes and numbers if you bust his ass for me
That is worst than getting kids lifted off a blunts stringed and laced so come explain ya revolution ill kindly sit and wait I'm always partial to an argument or intellectual debate
Now what you're giving me is a twisted bastard prelude to catastrophe
So ill purchase two vowels buy the letters A & E
Then toss them into the concoction they help spell out blasphemy
Almost as wild as telemarketing agents soliciting surprise weddings
And hospice showers for the terminally ill
U R utterly, ridiculous on second thought dispiteous
Poetry will be mine
Although I am really getting sick of this so back to some purposeful significance
DAYYYYUUUUUUMMNNNNNNNNNNNNNNN
Shawty up in tha front row fine lil mama body went off aye red aye girl aye woof woof
Cum hurr lil mama roll witta real nigga
Oh you a dime piece
Slide me yo digits bidisss

Almost as if hounding hoes is an infallible method of success in similar circumstances almost as if HEY LIL GIRL WANT SOME CANDY
Isn't played out
What I'm waiting for is the day where little girls call out to molesters to say ELEMENTARY DEAR WATSON! That shit is too cliché
And with a sense of pride and confidence goes on to walk away
But fuck it though you hoes love it though hows this example of tragedy
Exhibit A
Stunning sista mid teens honey hot super fly any choice of any guy and id hate to whine but we all know why, HE BROKE MY HEART
ALL I EVER WANTED WAS A MAN THAT WOULD MAKE ME HAPPY MAKE ME SMILE AWWW
Why does this keep happening to me????? Wahhh
What you didn't know is that she swore she would tame exhibit B
Hes the all star stud valedictorian of his class when passersby walk past they got enough

Exuberance to gasp his entire life is the epitome of the nonstop blast hes the biggest asshole in town straight tossing geeks in the trash and not to mention hes got the principle kissing his ass this chick thinks she can phase him?
What a foolish task her heart is broken again the shards be broken like glass In years passed I would felt for her this time ill just laugh !
These are the progressive thoughts of a child... of God who no longer bears foolish questions, for he has found his answer for the moment
His only struggle being that of memorizing play lines fresh rhymes high scores on Xbox live staying high in general managing a substandard algebra grade keeping his favorite girl interested + stepping his grown man game up, slowly but surely. He has found that love is crystal clear diamond of imagination found only in the movies

Autumn

Red rose, dead poet
Death by sweater weather wind
Blood thin brain frozen

I WOULD HAVE RATHER BEEN A CAVEMAN WITH A PLAYSTATION 2

DO YOU LIKE YOUR WOMAN SKINNY? WITH NO MEAT ON HER BONES OR THICK ABOVE AVERAGE AND BEAUTIFUL?

HAIKU MASTER

Question!
Has it been the views of everyone on life or a growing society that has kept this ever developing world restricted to the penalty of love?
I remember when love was a good thing. They just don't make em like they used to

It's 5-10-25 to life and nothing but a shallow whisper and a two hour conversation
A buzzing news crew and a rowdy school
Cameras and eyes aimed at the scene of the crime but the real criminal lingers just off set around the corner from the action. Wielding handcuffs instead of wearing them. Shoving innocents into squad cars instead of suffering themselves
Lenses aimed at crazed students begging them to rage antagonizing and egging them on until they finally snap! So we say no one can see into the eyes and minds of a criminal and of course it would be too late to ask the victim so we ask why can't it stop?
Why, why can't we just live the simple life and be free from fear hatred crime injustices poverty and discrimination racial and any

Erik Thomas

other kind! That's why I felt I would sacrifice and make the kind of statement that puts an end to the craziness of the world around me.

Upon much consideration I can't we as people have no way to prevent someone from fighting stealing harming one another

It's simply too much ground to cover and I have moved it into the realm impossibility

You can limit the outrage to an extent but truly can never defeat it

So this is why I would have rather been a caveman with a PlayStation 2

Free of caring loving and society too and not only would I be chilling with nothing to do I would still have a fully operational console game system too!

Think about it cavemen were labeled as primitive uncaring nomads real vicious people

And they still only watched out for themselves despite whatever clans they traveled with they had no love obligations or family to tend to. No one cares about their welfare or life hmmmmm... A carefree warrior with a ps2

Well I'm living in a fucking cave what the fuck else would I do?

Might as well have fun and wouldn't you too?

And that targets question dos

Simple and plain as 2 + 2 but with careful consideration it may prove to be true? Wouldn't you like to be able to live carefree without the reality and pain of another holding you down, not to feel pressed to wanting to know if Mommy's calling tonight? Not to feel that if Daddy doesn't pull around the corner tonight I may never see him again. People worry, and that's why alleviating this kind of pain would benefit not only people but wreck and crumble and ever criticizing society. I would have rather been a caveman, ahem question #3 too! One, if you think long take a deep breath and maybe count up to two being a caveman sounds good to me right...

How about you?

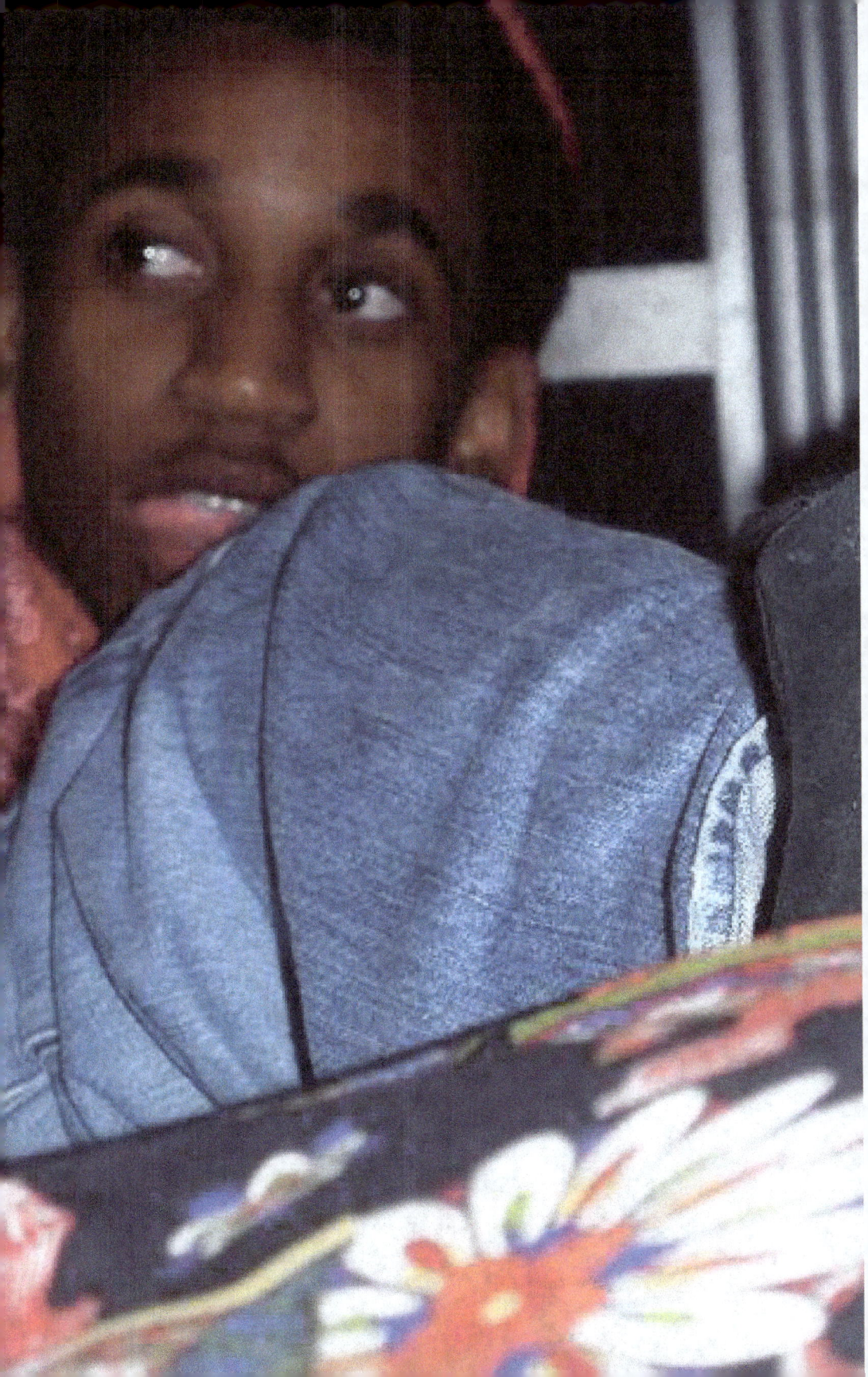

Autumn

Red rose, dead poet
Death by sweater weather wind
Blood thin brain frozen

PROPER BALANCE

CAN YOU FEEL ME IN YOUR LOWER EXTREMITIES OR AM I ONLY FOUND IN YOUR HEART AND YOUR MEMORIES?

Question/Statement! Whatever!
Actually never mind a Statement

Life does not have to resolve in tragedy. It's tragic, yes this has been said, it's been said again, but I'm here to explain how. Have you ever considered reconsidering before you thought about it twice?
Or ever stopped to realize that a nice life has a price?
For some, pessimism is not only a view but a principle or way of life they have been driven fully through!
Even though I always see my glass is filled half full I would never believe that because then I'd play the fool.
Although as time goes on your glass won't change no not one bit but as time goes on your soon to see that glass deserves a sip. First a sip then the thirst kicks in and you'd kill for just one more
But true hunger deserves a feeding to which the likes you must implore
Gotta eat.
Take a seat now you are patiently, waiting for it... for supper... you don't even really care what it is so you search life for that slice waiting for something anything and still nothing
Now you're straight window shopping for problems or at least a plate since nothing
Seems to be happening U psyche urself up you say yo ill make it happen B!
But its plain to see that a straight catastrophe is happening so naturally yet factually the curtains closing rapidly
Shows over faster than Eminem videos on BET
So then you see the brighter side the lighter side the politer side where obi wan swings lights outside and can dance the night away, but then you start to feel like Anakin with dark and conceited thoughts
With cruel intentions your evil premonitions
Therefore create your foul plots
You're the bad guy now and everything seems to slip right into place like when Velma shouts out Jinkies in one of Scooby Doo's mysteries
Its Yin vs, Yang, Good vs, Evil, Blood vs Crips, X-men vs Magneto
Pizza vs cheeseburgers times what nachos is to salsa dip or doritos every negative a positive and that's understandable but the success outside basic principles could cost your whole right hand
In the end for Caesar all was said was "eh tu brute?" My favorite dying lines heard up to this very day. A final thought a final word closing poetry, actually na fuck that shit! Ain't gon be no "..eh tu.." for me

This is my Proper Balance

Winter

*High frequency speech
Nothing colder than deep space
My heart & my tongue*

THE NIGHTMARE SONG

CAN YOU PLEASE,
PASS THE KNOTTY HEAD AND ORANGE JUICE?

HAIKU MASTER

Shit, I will abort.
I cannot afford to go forth without your support... forever yours ...mi amor
Mon Amie soon you'll see, that what we were, ain't half as much as what we'll be...
Ill raise the rivers, move the moons, and then I will separate the sea...
I would ward off all your demons while you rest easily for the rest of eternity...
I'll show you exactly what I've become, If you'd come stand here next to me.
I need you love, don't walk away... open your eyes and soon you'll see. What we were ain't half as much as what we'll be

 just you n me...

I could tell you stories of how personal eulogize,
Slay their owners will, and eventual rationality,
How half-filled trophy stands unbalance whole mentalities,
Shattered dreams and what-ifs from precedent realities,
All-star aspirant depressed, from harsh formalities,
Try to fulfill the stature you once held down like gravity,
Pause in disbelief and draw the motivation from outta me,
Petrified and solidified by the ghost of tainted vanity,
Watch it as it slowly departs, as a spirit within
Astonished by its past beauty yet you fear it again
Attempt to comprehend,
Without your bottle of Gin,
Watch recurring images and disheartened reveries spin,
See a distorted reflection,
Of what you could have been,
It taunts you provokingly yet seems so unearthly common,
And realization of what you've become, becomes the problem,
Your closest allies taking the blame, though you see it's not them,
You apply the pressure to their embodiment in order to defend,
Personal faults and bad calls on individual sin,
Eat yourself alive, and...Nooo... Not even then
Will, you be able to forgive the beast incarnated within.

I could be your worst dream, or best nightmare
Provoke the tension in your sleep, for one nights scare
R.E.M... Becomes the product of enticed fear
The pain inflicted on your person is realized here...

Erik Thomas

Prepare to embrace the terror,
Until your karma card is called
Your transformation begins, and then you see it's all your fault
Frightening instances attack you, breath becomes short
Try salvaging the final sip of a Tanqueray quart
It's your last resort
Before your body hits the floor,
Trepidation overcomes you and these images contort
Terrifying demons feasting on your flesh for sport
Shut your eyes, and come to realize the zombified assault.
Severed arms, a shattered skull, before your soul's spirit, will fall
You've recovered consciousness, but if not only just to stall,
Inevitable consumption of, what you've protected with your all
More than blood and sweat put in for the sake of this cause
A precious keepsake
Or story that's been told
A fable past down for the strongest and the bold
Bask in failure because you were unable to withhold
The power in order to keep significance of a secret untold
Before your final inhalation may you whisper the words?
The sacred, unheard,
For the sake of what you will have learned,

[He said]
"With development of passion may the will of love be concerned, ignorance spurned and all else of importance adjourned, may your desires oppositions take proper course and be torn, alleviate the guilty conscience of another bridge burned"
And with that said!
The wick of your entire life is burned,
A story once yearned, has now developed a major plot turn
In which the grounds of its outcome leave our hero's life worn…

I could be your worst dream, or best nightmare
Provoke the tension in your sleep, for one nights scare
R.E.M… Becomes the product of enticed fear
The pain inflicted on your person is realized here…

HAIKU MASTER

Departed,
Deceased,
In which you would be pleased to hear
It is in your best interest
To protect the bearings of your destiny
May your secrets and wills invest in me?
The guardian of what is left to see
The custodian of calligraphy
The scribe of symbolic meaning
Put your faith in something other than chances taken on a swift whim of heart
At which point do you decide to start
Taking pride in what you believe in,
Using prior knowledge to ensure that you are never deceived

in The beginning steps taken toward what you dream for
May you let your dreams soar!
Without clipped wings
And blocked paths
Just step pass
The boundaries set by mental stress
And profess
That you are ready to begin your final conquest
Take pride in your dreams…
Take pride in your destiny…
Thank you…

Winter

High frequency speech
Nothing colder than deep space
My heart & my tongue

GUYS LIKE ME

IS ONE WEEK TOO SOON TO BUY A GIRL A VALENTINES DAY GIFT?

HAIKU MASTER

"**Welcome to America**" land of missed opportunities, misperceived judgment, venomous slander, terrible self-esteem, unbearable prejudices, pathetic intentional defamation, un-wanted hesitance, and the plain fear of another human being. I mean. It's said…that **"Life is a Game"** but, somewhere along production in the software studio back behind the scenes some dick neglected to run a backup sweep and happened to miss a few glitches. Because my game doesn't seem to be playing correctly….or, maybe my controllers busted or something….but seriously what about the people so harshly deprived from the enjoyable essence of that **"Good ol' American Dream,"** I mean Life everyone lives it to the best of their ability **"Liberty"** is a term, lightly used amongst the masses, to persuade themselves they've got their passes, while emancipation is driven up their asses, with handcuffs and stand-ups as an answer to your restricted access you get nothing. But, a closer look at the bigger picture, which you decide to display obnoxious indifference with just because the quality exceeds your ability.

But the **"Pursuit of Happiness"** …man damn, that just throws an unfriendly screwdriver into my cranks, puts a blotch, in my ink, tosses the baby, out of my cradle, but FUCK analogies…let's think! Who of my mutual audience, would be a potential millionaire if you had a buck for every time you felt that you'd done something so personally offsetting that you felt you could blame yourself till the day you died? It feels kinda lame, just from someone who would know what lame felt like. I mean, what tha fuck? Misfortune is common amongst men, but then again…why does it seem so simple to peer into the lives of others and perceive nothing but common wealth, cheery faces and good health, flawless bodies and what else, parties, drinking, friends, girls, guys, sexy, lascivious imaginations the type of lives that I could only dream to fantasize, because the door to these opportunities is shut, like the chances of you reaching out to grab one of those stars from the sky, and though its helpless to try, you'd risk your life, or you'd die, for 15 seconds of that glamorous high. And, who tha fuck knows why? Because chances are, you'll hate where you're going, and you might not fit in, you might trek through this world committing every pleasurable sin, to the point of breakdown, and fucking erosion. Internal commotion, which kills your devotion, stress your emotion, until your tears fill the ocean, and begin over flowing…from over the side of Columbus's flat green EARTH, into an intergalactic black hole like pool of regret, and sorrow….but you wanted in. Sometimes, the best situation is the one that you're already in. Rejecting hoe's and dumb fools, like rubber to glue, that shit's lodged onto me, and stuck to you too!

Erik Thomas

Man...I probably couldn't even bare listing all of the things I am "**too!**" and.... just for personal reference, I'm talking "**too**" spelled Tee-Oh-oh, that 3 letter adverb defined as 'also' or 'besides' and, this way too strenuous to bare, but let's ride! **I'm TOO black, too white, too dumb, too smart, too slow, too fast, too lame, too gay, too hesitant, too indecisive, too skinny, too ugly, too cheerful, too depressed, too obnoxious, too out loud, too punk, too hip-hop, too emo, too friendly, too distant, too arrogant, too prude, too quiet, too tall, too short, too busy, too involved, too complicated, too perfect.....uh....TOO PERFECT!?** Too this? Too that? **3, 2, 1, two, I AM TOO**, fucking cool, for you, DAMNIT! This is driving me crazy! It honestly seems like, outside of all of my biological faults the only thing "right" about me is "he's really easy to talk to and he just has the nicest smile" shit, I'd rather cut out my tongue, and knock out all of my teeth, than have to face the mirror reflection of miserable disbelief. I mean, honestly... half the time, I feel like the odds of finding someone at a level headed frequency with me, are slim to none. I'm completely done with going against my desires to believe that the world isn't full of bullshit and let downs, may the spirits of hopeless romantics drown in a puddle of rejection, and give valiant resurrection to the spirits of brave hearted souls, with an achievable destination in liberties cruel world. With the wholehearted purpose of speaking for the sake of teaching, may I thank you for letting me find my proper balance, in with nirvana, extracted from the depths of the unknown beneath my trachea for nothing more than speaking several sentences, strength, solidity, significance, a starlit solitary, synthesis that is made possible by you, you make it seem so fucking splendiferous. While I seemingly couldn't pull the farthest thing from a dime, on a scale of one to ten, I'll be enjoyable to the effort that I display from here on in. Because while I watch my opportunities come and go like a tube of toothpaste in a four family two bedroom single bathroom home, I thrive in and live for the moments that I may share a bit of knowledge and make my story known. Take this as sincerely scribbled, for guys like me....

Thank you.

Winter

*High frequency speech
Nothing colder than deep space
My heart & my tongue*

IN THE END, IT IS FEELING THAT COUNTS

DOES GOD HAVE A RECORD BOOK OF EVERY GIRL I HAVE EVER KISSED?

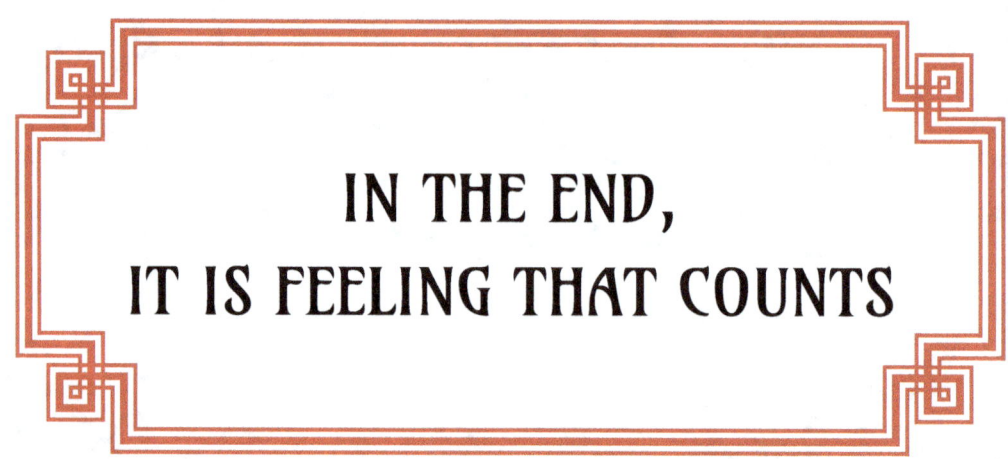

HAIKU MASTER

I'll leave your whole fucking perception gushing
Like you split your lip licking clit
So now yo shit is straight disgusting
Like, venereal-contaminated meets obscene-without-aggression
& you would have sworn her hips were legit
When she was slippin out her dress & then
Completely lusting, caught in cupids clutch and
Didn't even feel it necessary to let her return the brain before she busted
Now when you smile
I'm convinced your lips are sick syphilis infested
V.D. structured
Rotten rusted
Acne combusted
Sour genital repercussion
That has shattered your physical appearance and is now a psychological
o-b-s-t-r-u-c-t-i-o-n
Hardly the type of shit you could fix by mixing Robotuson
And I hope you learned yo fucking lesson
You see and this was intertwined with a bitch that you trusted
You have failed at life and lose at natural selection
If it were me I'd leave her carcass wrapped up in the dust bitch
End of discussion

Winter

High frequency speech
Nothing colder than deep space
My heart & my tongue

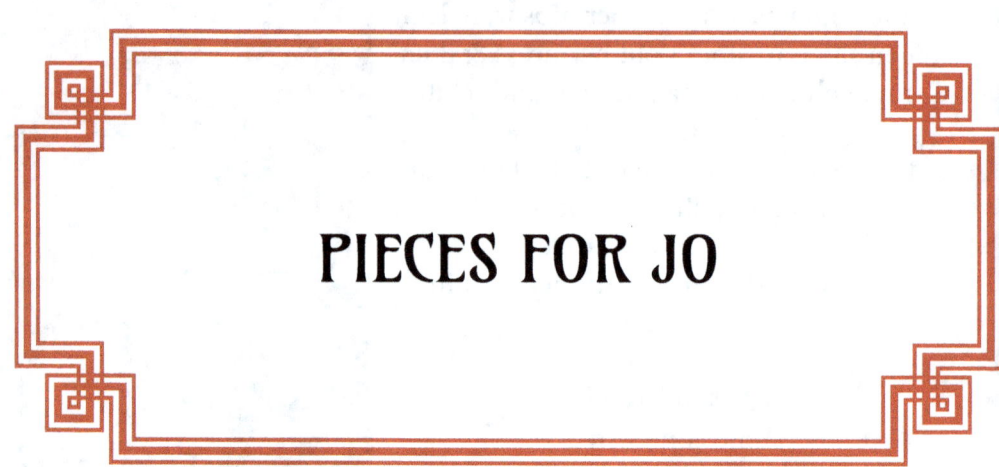

PIECES FOR JO

IS THERE STILL A WAY TO PLAY YOUR HAND FOR THE WIN WHEN YOUR QUEEN IS HIS ACE?

HAIKU MASTER

Stagnant Stagnant stares drawn forth by soulless men
Constantly wondering in drab despair whether or not they will ever get but a glimpse of light from the day.
Open and let your lungs breathe to suck up a fresh breath of air.
Unlatch the binding strings seaming from bare palms.
Puppet, bitch to master, a disaster. The crafter. Hypnotist with a vengeance consumed by laughter.
Dance Puppet, Dance! If I may?
A Story, A Stolen sketch
A complicated jest
And I would only cease to rest
After you truly do profess
Your love to me with no contest
Then I can caress your mind body soul & chest
And we can chill be together
But I only need a chance
Although this possibility can seem so distant and far away
Don't think that there is a time hour minute or even second of the day that I don't hope wish and dream of a future with you and me.

Erik Thomas

Here I am writing to that same girl again by now I've past confessed that I wanted to be more than just a friend
Maybe I'm a fool to want you so very badly, but I've thought and thought and thought to the point of driving myself mad.
You I want, you I would do most anything to have but I'm pretty tired of you throwing these painful punches and jabs..

Well here I am writing just scribbling lines, I could have sworn #8 would have worked just fine and I guess you figure already, this marks number 9 maybe my last pathetic attempt to woo you with rhymes hopefully my creativity will serve me better this time

Here I am standing with this girl she turned from that chick across the room to entire element of my world it has become difficult to explain a very complicated jest

And I, could only cease to rest
After, you truly do profess
Your love to me, with no contest
Only then could I, caress your mind body soul chest

But until then we can chill and be together. No matter how hard. The time has passed since I confessed… that I wanted to become more than just a friend and you kind of just gaped at me and said **"okay, weirdo keep dreaming!"**
Im paining myself for what seems to be no apparent reason cause it's like charging forth in a war that's been ten years past lost
I could swear it every day, on my body soul and life that in about twenty years someone like you will be my wife
You are a gorgeous intelligent humorous girl I can't understand how easily I become tense in your presence and the very whisper of your voice weakens me. I'm so remarkably frantic actually a little more upset that this couldn't come off more romantic
I mean this is supposed to be a love letter to this girl a display of sensitivity and the key to her dimension of the world and here I am writing what seem to be lame points and attempts…

I know you don't care much for religion but god damn girl you are blessed. And I do want to explain but it's a complicated jest and I would only cease to rest after you truly do profess your love to me with no contest only then would I caress your mind - body, body - soul, soul and breasts and we will chill and be together my heart you will possess
And I know it's pretty odd when I just stop talking and freeze stare into space like an idiot but you must see I'm collecting my speech. I'm actually as a loss for thought whether you believe it or not I feel so embarrassed and hot when I get put on the spot

I know it seems more like a confession but this was meant to be a love letter to this girl, she has turned from that chick across the room to this entire element of my world
Pieces For Jo

Sun	Moon
Drugs	Drugs

Sun Drugs
Moon Sobriety

Sobriety

ELITE

What's your fantasy?

DADAIST

DADA is what you can make out of...

DADA is not an art form

EXPRESSIONIST

I'm not as ill as...

oppose DADA

Deception vs Truth

WRECK

I don't slay tha living..
..I revive tha dead.

Winter

High frequency speech
Nothing colder than deep space
My heart & my tongue

SOGNARR #1 AKA I WANT IT TO COME NATURAL

I KNOW I'M OVER-DOING IT BUT IS IT TOO MUCH TO SAY, "I WANT IT TO COME NATURALLY?"

HAIKU MASTER

Sometimes I can't express my feelings and deepest emotions
Like how when I see you my heart drops, it's like it stops flowing
I don't know if my blood senses you and comes to halt
But when I can't even say hello, I feel it's my fault
And I don't know if it's your reaction that I'm scared about
I'd hate to approach you, make you angry, and have you start shout
Dear summerofcyclin
Love Sognarr

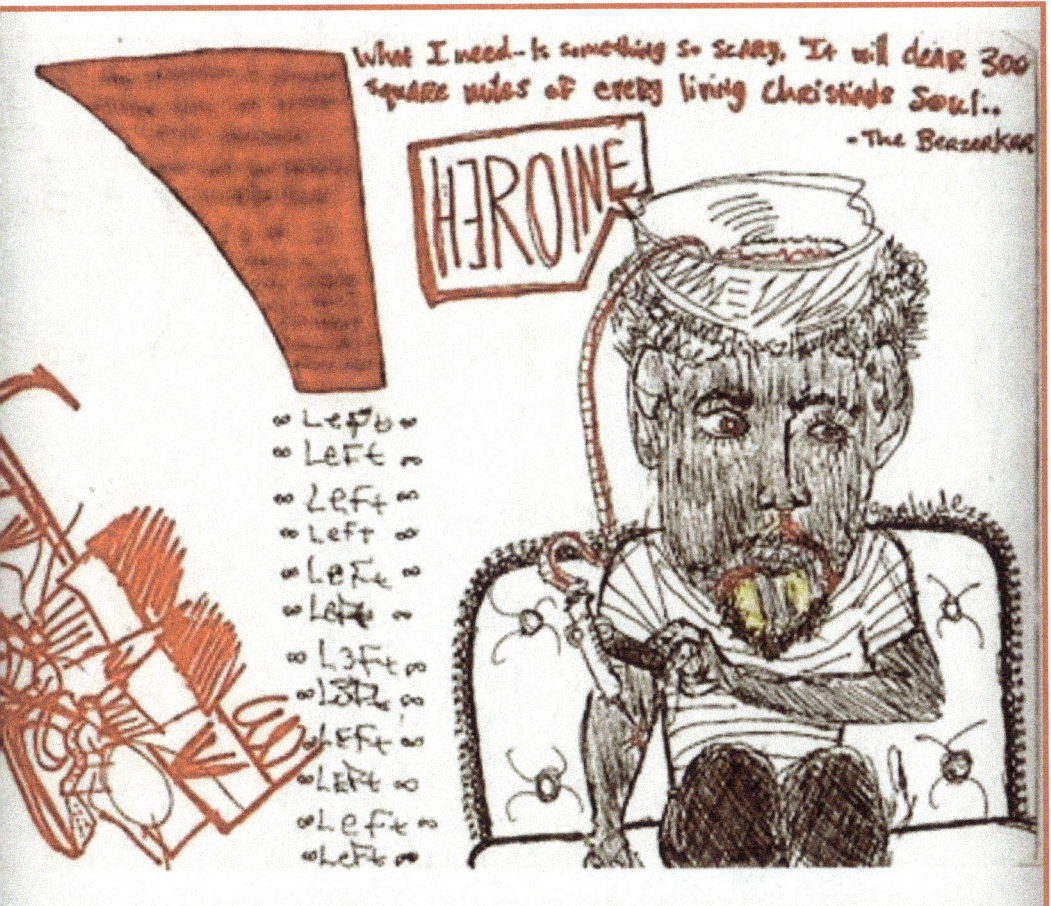

Winter

*High frequency speech
Nothing colder than deep space
My heart & my tongue*

IS TODAY A SAFE DAY TO SAY, "WE'LL BE FRIENDS FOR LIFE?"

HAIKU MASTER

From Phoenix: To Erik

The Poetry u bring 2 my everydaii blows away the black cumbersome
cloud that hangs above my head.
I adore your way with words, and how you put passion in the dullest of subjects.
Melodious is your dialect.
It rides through my head like a kiddy roller coaster looking straight ahead.
Dead ahead.
Silence falls on us both but our eyes won't stop talking.
Up up up the hill we go will we ever come down?
I'm not sure I want to know

Love: Phoenix

VIA VOCAL TONES

And that May, Trigger Dismay to 'Diss-Me'
When perplex situations just seem to convince me
That the point of existence is to 'Conflict' go against me
'Hesitation' makes my intentions 'Ris-qué'
Conflicting Considerations Close collapsing walls of my ribcage
When I engage in these anti-depressant tasks with a lit face
To shield hate, this vast mask crafted to seal fate
Consumed with the idea I bite my tongue in distaste…

Erik Thomas

IN A FLAWED WAY...
...MY MIND MAY
JUST DECAY...
...AND SEAL AWAY THE REMAINING REMNANTS OF A GOOD DAY.

If all that was desired of my existence was the '**GUST**' to blow away your
'black cumbersome cloud'
Just tell me now, I'd be more than happy to 'just' turn around
Without a **SHADOW** of a doubt, you've been the best that I've found,
I'd give my life up for yours…
…And I'll take my word to the ground
I've got this…Kiddy Roller Coaster revolving around the walls of my head…
…I'd like to analyze its 'metaphoric meaning', but I'll 'just ride it' instead
If it weren't for the silence, that falls over you and me,
I wouldn't inexplicably be scribbling this poetry,
So that ours 'eyes' would take a break,
And maybe your heart would notice me
But, ineffably, that's just the essence of romancing so hopelessly
MAYBE, I'LL SHOW THE RESONANCE OF MY DEPRESSION A LITTLE MORE NOTICEABLY?
I could, lash out with loud sounds, to drown out the thoughts in my head,
Let the publicity stunts falter a bit, Materialize my own world
Make our connection more physical,
A visual representation of a romance that's so chemical…

I… try… to tell her… that I love her. with barrages and arrays but when I ask her if she loves me she tells me not today.

I have found that the best method of forgetting you it is sleep because now I only think of you every forty seconds instead of every three.

Winter

High frequency speech
Nothing colder than deep space
My heart & my tongue

MY PHOENIX

IF LISTENING IS THE HIGHEST FORM OF RECOGNITION,
WHAT IS IT TO TRULY UNDERSTAND ONE ANOTHER?

HAIKU MASTER

    The legend of the Phoenix is as old as time. It's the tale of a bird burning itself every 500 years in order to renew its immortality.
    When in times of lackluster and unfurnished days, they rest invulnerably upon the flames that they create. And from the ashes of the old weary Phoenix, the new flawless beautiful Phoenix is born. By overcoming fire, death, and old age an outstanding symbol of triumph over adversity and rebirth into glory provides true hope and constancy to all in the Phoenix's reach…

    The legend of the loser slash hopeless romantic is unexpectedly just as old, if not older than the Phoenix itself. The tale of a young lad that faces countless trials of professing true love and is often times placed against all odds in his quest to find the diamond of his day. Well, I'd hate to bore you and disinterest you with prefaces and prologues, so may we let our tale begin…

    Allow me to transport your mind's eye into a world, where walls don't exist…
Where water flows upward, and oxygen is nothing but a priceless delicacy
A world where the faces of random passersby are constantly cheery to the point of intolerable self-confusion…and oh how I hate cheery random passersby.

Erik Thomas

Where unbirthday parties occur lively and are accepted 363 days out of the year…the even two left out belong to the only people that matter in this section of this little world, but you're more than welcome to explore your own semi dimensions…in order to find your personal delight… I'd like to be able to say, that I can take credit for the creation of this place, but I didn't do it alone…

"If I had a world of my own, everything would be nonsense. Nothing would be what it is, because everything would be what it isn't. And contrary wise, what is, it wouldn't be. And what it wouldn't be, it would. You see?"

-Alice

It was in the very essence of this need to impress,
That the perplexity of his state became essential to address,
He been lost and not found, left unbound and distressed,
When he sought out a means of how to profess,
He let the pen do the talking, at which ink point he could blame.

The dame that he sought for, was now lost to the game…
His head unexpectedly burst into flames
Mentality and reality inversed on a plane
From delight and pleasure, to regret and shame
Revolving hourglass effect, watching the hours of his life that it claimed
Wasted, without reason, conscious to the fact that he was playing a game

An unarmed, untrained member of a losing infantry
He let the chorus tell him too many times that he'd write her a symphony
Now he sulked in humiliation indifferently
His sonata incomplete without a last taste of her desirability
Waning for a impulsive reminiscence of her memory
Then the feral inferno vanished swiftly
Now he stood center stage in a tumultuous rage
Confused past the point of surreal time and age
Apparently lost in his thoughts, obviously on the wrong page
As he observed his surroundings, he noticed he'd been encaged

He wanted to be angry, but then his voice was misplaced

HAIKU MASTER

Discovery of self-became all that seemed it should matter,
Who, what, when, where, why, how had this happened
[He couldn't hear himself talk, and though he swore he was speaking,
The only audible sound derived from the voice of a beacon]
Suddenly an array of bright light shot from out of the ceiling
His temporary confinement began automatically unsealing
Just then, a vision of her became all that was real…
The ground literally vanished…and she literally became all he could feel…
His addiction for her smile was now fulfilled once again…
So, he fiendishly reached for a pocket and pen…
This sensation of inspiration then he's lost in the wind…
On a cool winter day, by the lake, where they slept…

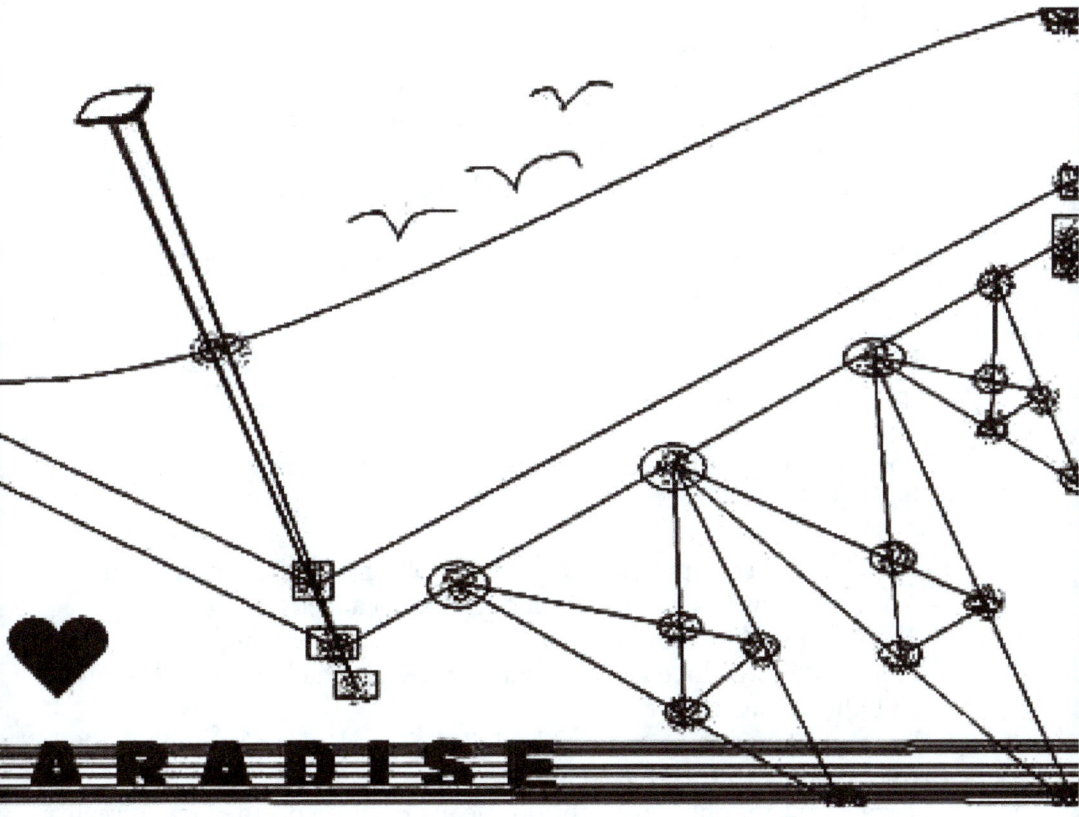

Erik Thomas

Her nestled comfortably on an uncomfortably damp padded landing pit beneath a makeshift half field goal post, half pole vault type bar formation that's inept…

He couldn't imagine how he was placed in this situation sitting with this perfect girl, in the perfect instance of life, at the perfect time …it was about twenty minutes past sunset…

When he should have probably had his mind on the twenty mosquitoes that were sucking the 'perfect life' from his neck…

When the sun slipped right over the horizon, and the surreal impact of a potential dilemma became relevant, he kept his mouth shut and hit the pause button.

She froze…
He sat there and examined her embodiment and pose…
Scrutinizing the hi-lights in her hair, and the form of her toes…
The irresistible beauty of her eyes when she stared,
And the whiskers under her nose…
He analyzed, to search for whatever he thought he might find in her eyes

His exploration devoted to any surprise, or secret he might find looking into those eyes…

Mesmerizing, astonishing, unbelievable…they consumed his thoughts, dreams, and in this still instance…he wished…

For the pause button to be released, so he may receive his long awaited kiss…

But, then pressed play, and realized another opportunity missed…
And soon saw his mistake, when he then realized
That without her in his life, he'd be miserable many nights
Pain is love…or love is pain…and, given the chance id do all that bullshit all over again…
For the sake of being miserable right here today, scribbling line after worthless line with this digital pen…
Time and thought consumption means nothing on the face of reality,
When the gamble for love is made an improbable formality,
You should strive for your feelings, and even if you don't win

HAIKU MASTER

**You have the meaningful memories to guide you correctly
When you do try again…**

My Phoenix exists as an untouchable being…
Whose affection, when given to whomever she deems worthy,
Will inevitably create an indescribable sensation of fulfillment
An unmatched emotional enthrallment
As the days of our lives become more and less gradually content
I'll take my position as her key to a more promising life
As promised…
And keep hopes that this past version of love will recompense

Just know, that it is dreams, not reality that keep my expression of affection condensed
I can also pray that soon, I am convinced that there are other beings worth the same time and effort that I have put into this…

Signed by slash love
-Erik Thomas

p.s.

Life is like weed. When there is nothing left, all the people you used to smoke with will be gone and its just you left with an addiction you'll never kick and a void you will never fill… therefore smoking themselves and each other.

$pring

*Lately, I'm cordial
In tune with earths sensory
Scorched charms Gemini*

THIS TRYST

IF I CLOSE MY EYES TONIGHT WOULD YOU PROMISE ME YOU'LL SING ME TO SLEEP? GOODBYE – GOODNIGHT A LULLABY FOR LEAVING?

HAIKU MASTER

By: Erik Thomas

Precautions plague his thoughts as he prepares for this engagement,
The time in between these meetings has made his mind so incomplacent,
Secret rendezvous between these two has shifted placement,
He dreams of the exact instance, where his other half may stop replacing,
The bounds of a true relationship without the ties of complication,
He's grown to hate this game; at the same time he feels this captivation,
Wondering whether he'd even be able to survive without her fragrance,
Hopelessly bound to the very purpose of this admiration,
Fiending for just another touch or sensual sensation…
It's 11:14

He: Hey, look I know this has been going on, and without much problem for quite sometime, and its…*sighs* its been the most invigorating experience of my life…you, you, you are incredible…but this…I cant do this anymore.

She: I don't understand

He: I don't expect you to, I've thought this over… time and time again, and just contemplating to myself whether I'd ever see you again I was going to stay home! I mean, how can you figure that I don't think about you from time to time during my everyday life? Sometimes I sit waiting partly expecting a phone call from you just to ensure your alright, and I might fucking die if I don't see you next time, Its just, insane how we could have established these periodic meetings, I just don't understand… I…I want a chance to know who you are…that's all I'm saying…can I take you out for some coffee sometime?

She: Look, I cant… its just not possible, to be honest, you are constantly on my mind as well, I don't think that personal matters of my life are of any concern here at all, and though I would love to get to know you, I just don't think I can… things like that never turn out well with me, I just… I just want to try something new…

Erik Thomas

He: Something new? So, you put blame on your past relationships and instances where you've opened your feelings to anyone, and rely on that to guide you through your future… I just cant live with the fact that assholes, or anything in your past has prevented me from an opportunity with you, I just…need to know you…you have to understand that?

She: I do…I'm completely connected with you too, and it just seems like, a manner of secrecy is where I'm comfortable in life, you wouldn't like me anyways, trust me I'm completely unpassionate in every aspect of life, im a klutz, an unliked secretary at some bullshit newspaper, my life is just not interesting, and I just don't want to introduce you to things that I have no pride and self worth for…I CANT DEAL WITH THIS RIGHT NOW!! I hate to block out things that have possibility to be good for me…

HAIKU MASTER

He: So don't, I just cant live with that on my mind, and in life…'The best thing that ever happened to me' completely secluded from the rest of my life due to past experience, unable to show affection in any way other than sexually…it just, doesn't work for me…look, I'll accept you as you are, no stipulations, no lying, just full acceptance of who you are, and we can start from the beginning…

In that instance, she trembled…
Her fears stripped
Her heart fixed
The shards left lying amongst the pits of her stomach were instantly revitalized…
Her destiny was finalized…

And now with emotion, and not in the past 8 years did she let her body and mind embrace the possibility of something worthwhile…she realized
And that moment her real eyes shed tears for overdue cries,
His words with passionate meaning had actually symbolized,
The recognition of her happiness
So, without a moment's time spent, he basked in this
This final tryst
This sewing stitch
To mend this bitch!
Past a point of happiness that was unmatched by any sustaining lifestyle she had encountered in the past…

Never after, Happily is how this story ends….

$pring

*Lately, I'm cordial
In tune with earths sensory
Scorched charms Gemini*

HIM & HER

FLY GIRL FROM BROOKLYN WHEN THEY ASK YOU HOW YOU KNOW ME WOULD YOU PLEASE TELL THEM I STARTED AT THE SEA FLOOR AND SURFACED SLOWLY

HAIKU MASTER

Negative connotation
A serious lack of worthwhile conversation
Grand surplus of masturbation
All because I was too involved with my PlayStation
Late bloomer
No relations
Prolonged prerequisites and hesitation
Seemingly, no consolation
To the dick that's so impatient
Yet, gets no penetration
With unlikely, integration
Receiving no commendation
And missing vital compilations
Told by her to value patience
While he awaits with dedication
She speaks on love and harmonation
While he just seeks ejaculation
But he pleads… valid interrogation
While she secedes with exclamation
Forgetting her promise to her most valued patron
That has brinked to tears in complication
His heads straining in perplexation
While she contemplated with concentration
About her current most vocation
Love to her has signification
That wont be broken by impatience
She knows he truly loves her and wouldn't test her patience
They both desire this sensation
A virgin's eyes tell of consideration
To years of sentimental vacation
Conquests for love on dream lit stations
REM plus infatuation
Leads to deathly sincere fascination
And though both boy and girl are complacent
Both he and she yearn for restoration
Of what was once their relation
Though without internal exploration
With each other as destinations
She gives him herself and they share a historical moment in their lives
Love is burned into their memory for eternal
Co-existence

$pring

*Lately, I'm cordial
In tune with earths sensory
Scorched charms Gemini*

METAPHORICAL WAY OF PERCEIVING YOUR CURRENT DILEMMA

TOO MUCH EMCEES NOT ENOUGH FANS
WHY EVERYBODY WANNA ROCK THE MIC
BUT NEVER WANNA CLAP THEY HANDS?

HAIKU MASTER

    Metaphoric perception allows the description of the topic to be embodied in a figurative entity, similar to the way I have characterized the elemental "**Phoenix**" of my life…
    Surprisingly, I haven't ever considered classifying any of my other daily trials in such a way, but I would just as easily find something perplexing to myself and create a symbolic relevance to the problem in which I find difficult to face.

    Time…that's probably the biggest word I've ever said, that's appalling based on the fact that I've got a vast amount of words inside my head… seconds that tick away the occasions in which I've missed opportunities without intent, if I dared state my desire to want time back I'd bask in the regret… self-lament, is what would ultimately result as consequence, in the event I broke my promise to live life without regret…Now this, is the component to my **enigma** in which you'll 'get' the part where comprehension of the preface becomes a lot less significant…

Erik Thomas

If I were to take the magnitude of "time" and stuff it into an hourglass, I'd end up scrutinizing the figurative image of "time" until the final hour passed, the substantial visual of the 'time' would in turn become the perception of your metaphoric tormenting task, until you took it upon yourself to shatter the fucking glass!

The only way to dismember the bounds of a metaphorical perception is to figure out the ordeal, and to solve your **enigma** of sorts…by finishing the tasks necessary to have complete understanding of the predicament.

HAIKU MASTER

Ex-> for me to complete my conquest of finding and keeping the **Phoenix** of my day, for me to fulfill my desires with her, and become truly happy on an affectionate and relationship type level. For me to have created the time ordeal and embodied my image of time in an hourglass, I would have to then understand the way it work, consequences of breaking my sole promises to myself, understanding scheduling and due process of life, only then would I be able to forget about or alleviate myself from the concept of the **hourglass.**

$pring

*Lately, I'm cordial
In tune with earths sensory
Scorched charms Gemini*

GREY

WHO CARES WHAT MOVES A FOOT SOLDIER MAKES? WILL YOU BE ABLE TO MAINTAIN COMPOSURE AT THE HEAD OF THE TABLE?

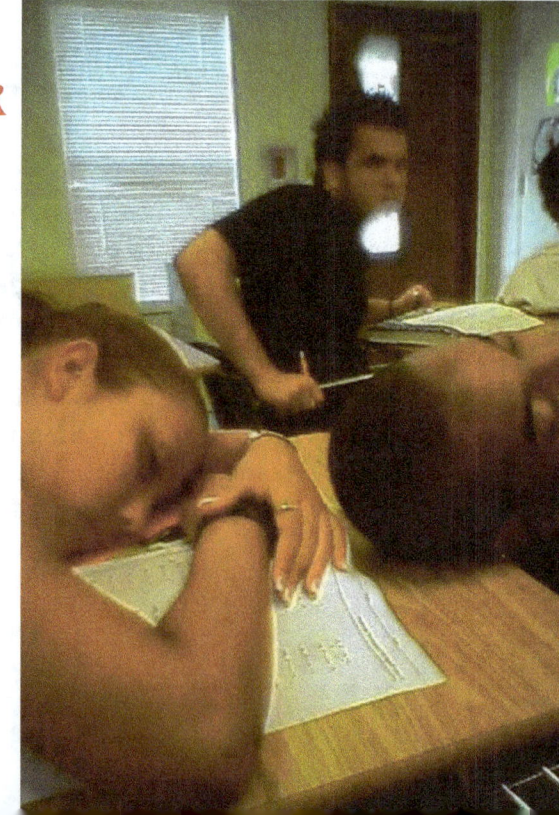

HAIKU MASTER

So, I'd be better off tatting the word Belligerent in ink across my face

Phonetic spelling across my chest and the definition around my waist

For anyone who won't judge me, without logical trial and case

Consider the worst possible circumstance, and begin to place some distaste, because my logistics show you the story of a more malevolent disgrace in which my character overcame me, and I couldn't stand to embrace.

TO BE THE OUTLYING SOURCE OF COLOR TO PROVIDE FOR YOUR WORLD OF GREY

I'll show you the duplicity that you left wickedly when you laid that kiss on me, if you would only see the days I have gone through with my mind racing viciously, it's sickening, how I could want you despite the continuous sympathy that I create when I'm upset and the hate portrayed when I get livid visibly, you think you've had it bad rephrase your tone, I could simply speak surreptitiously, silent but stealth songs would make my sirens dream become genuine, sue me I was made to win that's why my efforts became so completely persistent… though it's in my best interest to leave you alone I'd die before the day that I give in. I can manage though, I'll continue dreaming and fortifying my considerations, so that I overcome given the instance I'm¬¬ ever thrown into the situation, I'll have the reflection of self to just command hesitation… blame me if I come off just a little inconsiderate, and a lot less impatient…

Ill beat the clock before I stop given the right motivation. What words mean to me is golden; I'll put my love in a rhyme, create a correlating pulse then I'll straight defibrillate lines, check one two, clear resuscitated the base of what could have been mine, hip-hop dream is coming back I'll find my place here in time.

HAIKU MASTER

No opposition too difficult to face, I've been a disgraceful communist since before the day I was born, I was in the womb plotting global domination so that on Doomsday, June 8th, I would scorn. Love is only as complicated as you make, shit… I would rather make it complex, through the stress, through the pain that you suppress for success, when you're blessed and you vent through your pen, when its meant to be sent, through the airwaves, content when you've spent so much time on what's been given as a gift… one part passion plus a hint of ill grit becomes the formula base spit in order for a rhyme or event.

$pring

*Lately, I'm cordial
In tune with earths sensory
Scorched charms Gemini*

CAN YOU REALLY OPEN UP A PERSON AND SEE WHAT IS WRONG WITH THEM?

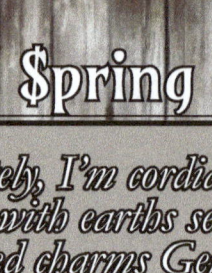

What constitutes a 'loon' from beneath the skin with a scalpel? When a lobotomy tortured fiend is diagnosed without ample
Support and devotion, inconsiderate attention leaves another life trampled
Classify the mass population as 'mad' without answer

Now presenting your favorite talk show host,
With thoughts so close to disturbed,
That most of his words are cheap shots that no one deserves
Lashing out on unprotected entities with malicious satisfaction
The verbal bully that makes you suffer the consequences without an action
Cause and effect directed with the most malevolent intent
Past irrelevant, I won't remain complacent until you bask in lament
Do you comprehend? …

That's fine, ill repeat it again…
I'm quite literally only pleased by your pathetic depression, your likely dismay allows my swaggering self-esteem to transcend
I'm the arrogant over competent… friend
That shows no compassion if you're lacking the ability to win
From the clean sole of my sneakers to the luster in my grin
Ill be the closest thing to your loving angel that has never neglected to sin…

One flew over the cuckoo's nest, Tragic as can be…
Dealt with insubordination, contention and brash sexuality
The basis of the story described as a harsh formality
Strict governing of men that wanted nothing more to do with fallacy
Ms. Ratched ran the psyche ward with a firm grip mentality
Unbalancing the mental stability of all admitted with brutality
Shock treatment without remorse rendered patients a step from a fatality
Chief Brodem lacking motivation and or a will to contend,
Until salvation in the form of Randle McMurphy stepped into the ring,
A guiding light to rescue faith came complete with ill-mannered tendencies,
Perverted the minds of the previously ill-minded
but also gave them potency
The vigor to persist
The power to stand strong on their own
Without inspiration from their hero they'd have been still under control…
GONE!

$ummer

Hibernation feel
Thawed iced leaves river bends
Lake beds and stretched limbs

INTERGALACTIC INTIMACY

WHEN YOU CANNOT HOLD ON ANY LONGER. WHEN IS THE RIGHT TIME TO LET GO?

HAIKU MASTER

WRAITHMATICIAN-

Looking at the solar system,
The planets glisten,
Open your heart and just start to listen,
I'll play Jupiter you can be mars,
We gunna shine brighter than all the moons and stars,
I've been known to be out of this world,
And shake cats with sick rap lyrical pearls,
So if you down for an E.T. experience,
Why not experiment,
With space ships and stations,
Skate through creation,
Straight through the nation,
Into orbit like lunar exploration,
NASA hunts for me cause I'm dancing on the Hubble, telescope to help cope with all of my troubles,
Been deep like great whites breaking at the surface,
Makin cracks on mommas backs as if there wasn't purpose,
I'm in deep space for the ninth time for clarity,
I keep coming back lookin for some sincerity,
I sit on Saturn's rings thinking all of these things and it starts to bring another broken memory scene,
But if it hits you hard promise me remember one thing,
No pain is more real than what a memory brings,
Dancing heart attack breakdowns for the broken kings men and horses,
A battlefield of divorces,
Wave your white flag and come count your losses,
Twenty to ten odds you'd be shaken up broads for a quarter to call a home

SOGNARR-

Watch her…
Intrigued by intergalactic imagery,
Sketched into infinity by superimposed energy,
Creating a visual balance of symmetry,
So, our hearts may co-exist with universal intimacy,
Rise! As I snatch stars from skies, insert them in her eyes,
In order to hypnotize, my proper balance upon this enterprise,
Lost in Space, my only mission is to synthesize,
A correlation of cosmic nights,
In which we might,
Become involved in aviated flight,
As we glide amongst the northern lights,
Only then would the existence of me & you be right
To stargaze on dark days
To lustfully lark blaze & spark haze while fortifying such an immense craze
Intense fades concentrated on familiarizing myself with your ways
& of course my pens fine
So keep the trim tight

This plight might be ideal
Regardless of or in spite of every wicked abusive
Illuminated confusion that's been bruising my mind at the expense
of quixotic contusions
If it were up to me we wouldn't still be choosin
I would make you the queen to my throne
The star to my sky
The dot to my "I"
The wings so I fly
The brightest diamond in a blood soaked pile,
Girl give me a chance, and just stay for a while…
We will face this conquest of, space and time…
Just put your hands in mine…
Just let your feelings ride…
Just…

Dream…let your emotions stream,
Across the seam,
Of the border to a greater being,
Joint together by a greater means
By the proper pronunciation of the letters … L-O-V and E

$ummer

*Hibernation feel
Thawed iced leaves river bends
Lake beds and stretched limbs*

YOU SAY "YOUR WRITINGS ARE SO PERFECT"

I NEVER AMOUNTED TO SHIT. I DIDN'T MAKE ENOUGH MONEY TIL I STARTED THINKING FUCK MONEY, HOW COME THE PEOPLE THAT HAVE MONEY TREAT MONEY LIKE THERE IS SO MUCH OF IT?

I say, apparently not...

Erik Thomas

If I didn't incorporate enough personal ideas that I intentionally tried to relate directly to my life, directly to our relationship **or our lack thereof one** then my writing was far from perfect. I was obviously able to describe and instance that was interesting enough to hook my viewer/reader but, the essence of my purpose was probably lost in the words… I guess, I'd hate for this to be an instance where it was something that has to be read times and times again for anyone to understand, not that I feel anyone else should be able to, but that wasn't what I intended for it to be. I guess, I took the idea of writing about a subject you had selected for me, as more of an intimate project, and never at any point did I even have a second thought that it would be about you. I kind of don't even want to read the one you wrote, for the fear that it doesn't say what I want it to, and I'm completely positive that it won't have anything directly involving me…and in the event that it does, I'm positive that whatever that explains isn't what I feel like I want to, or I need to hear.

ONE PIECE × somethin like a PIRATE

us like livin...

Ingenicus Insignicoo

its jus me, yo 4 hoes, and a bottle of rum

But it dont take myself to you...

.. Finish

> your!... & thats how it isz.

$ummer

*Hibernation feel
Thawed iced leaves river bends
Lake beds and stretched limbs*

DECEMBER 12TH, 2006, 09:31 PM:

WHAT DO ALL THE PEOPLE IN THE 27 CLUB HAVE IN COMMON?

"THE BIGGEST RAPPER IN HISTORY."

HAIKU MASTER

At which point...
Do we decide that we want to exist or co-exist above our words...
When, it becomes seemingly pointless for verbal conversation
Only based on the fact that, words won't be enough
When, actions begin to speak
Like mutated demons
Walking and seeing
Continuously screaming
And growing, with one purpose of being
To convey the message your soul seeks to be heard
Heard, and comprehended
Not complimented
Or befriended
Just understood by the only other person that matters
At which point
Should we face facts?
And react
To the impact
Of an empty wish unfulfilled till a later day
At which point
Do you hope and pray
That the inevitability of life takes place today
And that you may no longer have dream to wait
Deciding on whether to display patience or carry on in dismay
Unable to decide upon what should happen next
Or incapable of realizing whether it's even your decision or not...
At which point will I know....

Current Location: Mi Casa
Current Mood: hopeful

$ummer

Hibernation feel
Thawed iced leaves river bends
Lake beds and stretched limbs

THE NOVICE AND THE GODDESS

IF I COULD AFFORD TO PAY YOU TO FORGET ABOUT ME
HOW LONG WOULD IT TAKE BEFORE YOU CAME BACK?

HAIKU MASTER

      Dream, let your emotions stream…
…Across the seam of a border to a greater being
      Brought together by a greater means…
…The proper pronunciation of the letters L-O-V and E

Question…

      When was the last time you met your match…?
Let me explain, this object of sentiment who puts your whole mind intact, a sudden awakening within, you've gained the drive to catch, her eye at a moment's notice before your opportunity's left… out the door without a word, its almost unfair you see… you took a bit too long to

Allow me to take you on a voyage, I'll explain it vocally… a lesson learned amounts to greater meaning than the teaching of a soul with hope you see…?

      That… if you don't take me now, I'll have a heart attack love
My fatal convulsions worth us not spending time in fact love
That, I've gone past the point of return, **No Turning Back** love
Trapped in the depths of mental consumption without fates escape route skittle path love
There is no way to backtrack without your support Mon Amie
Soon you'll see that what we were ain't half as much as what we'll be…
I'll raise the rivers, move the moons, and then I will separate the sea…
I would ward off all your demons while you rest easily for the rest of eternity…
I'll show you exactly what I've become, If you'd come stand here next to me.
I need you love, don't walk away… open your eyes and soon you'll see.

      But then she whispered the truths of her dying affection toward his hoping presence without glee…her piercing words even dropped our hopeless hero to his knees…she said: "My time here has passed, and with your obtained knowledge, you'll undoubtedly soon be the most magnificent mind materialized and meant for the sake of love ever, over the course of history." He replied, fuck your stupid logic, just look at what you've done to me! Before he spoke another word, she laughed at his animosity… she said "I've given you the best ascension toward romantic divinity…how could you ever even almost deny the prospects of my wish to set you free…?" He staggered over his sentence, but he managed to get his point out clear and free… you've taught me how to 'think' and create all the

things that I do see… to recognize the bounds of one's desires and how to offer them their dreams… however, the one thing you haven't instructed was what I take in personally…my own essentials were never met, as well as the necessities… the one thing I've ever wanted was to make 'you' live so happily… you don't get it, I won't love again, this marks the end of me, you're all I've ever wanted, and you'll be all I ever need… I'll say it once more as your Romeo, Juliet please don't leave…?
I promise to God, if you walk out that door ill fucking cease to breathe…

    Her expression was unforeseen, she hadn't expected this… her perception on what she'd done here…and all for just a kiss? She couldn't quite see why he cared so much, or what she'd done to deserve this, she couldn't bear to see him loveless again… but she wouldn't suffer through the bliss… before she motioned to speak again, she noticed a wetness on her face… a single tear slid down her warming cheek, then she noticed her mistake… apparently she showed someone who had nothing, the most excellent virtues of what love could make… she altered an entire thought process, and then his heart was left to break, she cried the happiest tears she'd ever fathomed as he offered his hand once more to take… Then, the Goddess outreached her arm, with a bit of hesitation, how on heaven or why on earth had she created this revelation, surpassed amongst her own craft… shocked amidst his presence the creation… a mind's time consumption of true creativity is bounds for miraculous manifestation…

    A sound seconds slower than Saddam's Saudi Arabian invasion yet light years faster than a single inhalation pace placed to save face in case of cardiopulmonary resuscitation -- she went left, told him to close his eyes took a breath, blew a wind from her chest blessed with the rest of her best stuff summoning a gust that must have done it – Err sent our hero to plummet – **to death** by way of ripping the soul from his chest – He expected none less...

THE NOVICE & THE GODDESS

www.ingramcontent.com/pod-product-compliance
Lightning Source LLC
Chambersburg PA
CBHW071539080526
44588CB00011B/1727